DEDICATION

This book is dedicated to my wife, Faby, my son Eja and to all the parents of children on the autism spectrum who dare to go beyond the label.

To my friend Bam Bam whose patience and love of family inspire me every day.

Introduction

This is the first book in a series dedicated to exploring the beauty of autism and the diversity of intelligence in nature.

At the back of this book, you will find a version of this story written using the "Scratch Jr." coding language. I encourage parents to read the book with their children and then write the code to see it come to life differently.

All the proceeds of this book series go to "Autism Bird," a wonderful non–profit helping parents navigate the autism journey with their child. For additional donations, visit https://autismbird.org/.

For more information on Scratch Jr go to: https://www.scratchjr.org/

About the Author

Saikou Diallo is a teacher, scientist, and engineer who builds simulations for a living and works with children on the autism spectrum.

This first book in the series is a tale of Two Saikou. Saikou, the Elder who wrote the text, and Saikou, the younger who wrote the code. Both Saikou love reading, math, science, poetry, art, and sports.

Lenny walked to school every day. He loved to walk in alleys and side streets. He never took the same route to school because he liked discovering the big city and all its wonders.

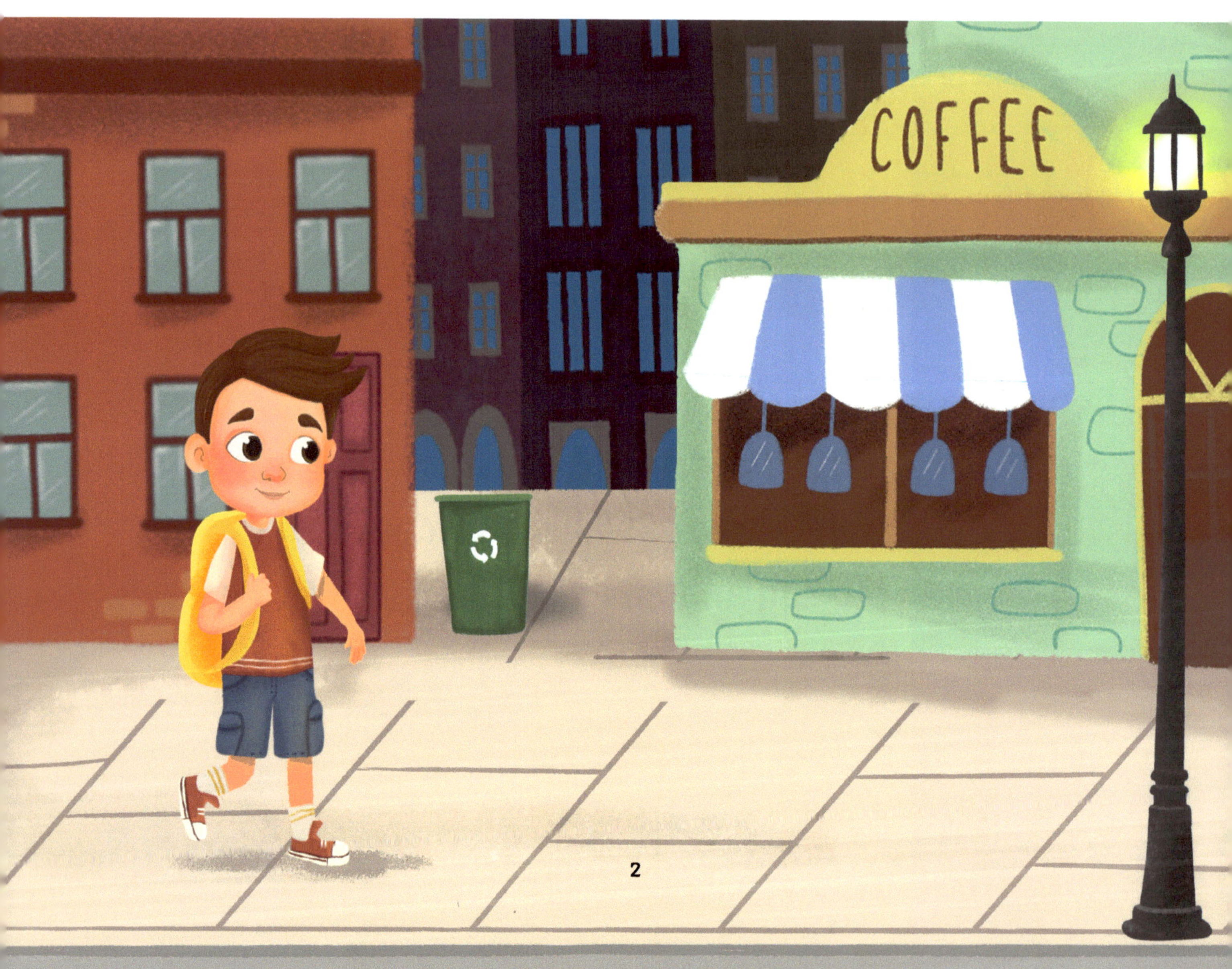

2

One day, down an alley, Lenny saw a black cat walking on his toes around a trash can.

How weird and wonderful, thought Lenny! I have never seen a black cat walking on its toes. Come to think of it, I have seen any cat walking on its toes.

He stopped ten feet from the cat and cleared his throat. "Excuse me, Mr. Cat! What is your name, and why are you walking around this trash can on your toes."

PIZZERIA
BOOK S

The cat ignored Lenny for a few seconds, spun in a ballerina—like pirouette three times, and finally said, "Bam Bam." Lenny waited to hear more, but the cat went back to spinning.

After a few more pirouettes, the cat said "People call me Bam Bam, but that is not my name. People ask questions, but they do not want to know."

ZZERIA
OPEN
BOOK
6

Lenny came closer and took Bam Bam's paw. He said "I do want to know, and I do want to learn. Tell me about you, and I will tell you about me, And then eventually, you and I can be friends."

Bam Bam stopped spinning and looked beyond Lenny with a gentle smile. He was happy that Lenny wanted to know him, but he did not know what to say.

ZZERIA
OPEN
BOOK
8

Bam Bam thought about it and said:
"Ok, let me tell you about me.
I am who I am, and I like what I like
I like to stim, and I like to spin
Sometimes people are afraid of me,
even though I am nice and friendly.
I can talk, but I prefer action
Some believe I am a genius
Others think I am an idiot savant
Either way, I am myself and nobody else.
" But, enough talk, let's just play."

PEN
10

Lenny wanted to ask more questions but did not know what to say. He wanted to talk about his favorite videogame and his prowess with the baseball team. He wanted to talk about his day, his mom, his teacher, and everything that went on at school. Instead, he smiled at Bam Bam and spoke. "Ok, let's play."

Lenny forgot all about school. He chased Bam Bam down the street and around the corner. He ran up alleys and under bridges with Bam Bam until darkness fell.

SCHOOL

It was time to say goodbye and go their separate ways. Bam Bam hugged Lenny and held him tight. He did not want to let his friend go because they had so much fun.

14

Lenny, too was sad. Although they did not speak, he had a ton of fun running with Bam Bam. He wanted to say many things and how much he enjoyed the day with his new friend. But he had learned a vital lesson.

Different people communicate differently.

He offered his fist, and they both said "Same time tomorrow!!"

16

Lenny and Bam Bam Code Together

Chat
Table de chevet
Enfant
Soleil
Ok let
I am
i like
Someti
event
i can
Some
Other
Either
But
10
4
3
2
3
2
3
6
2
10
20
24
Bam-
24
People
People
2
20

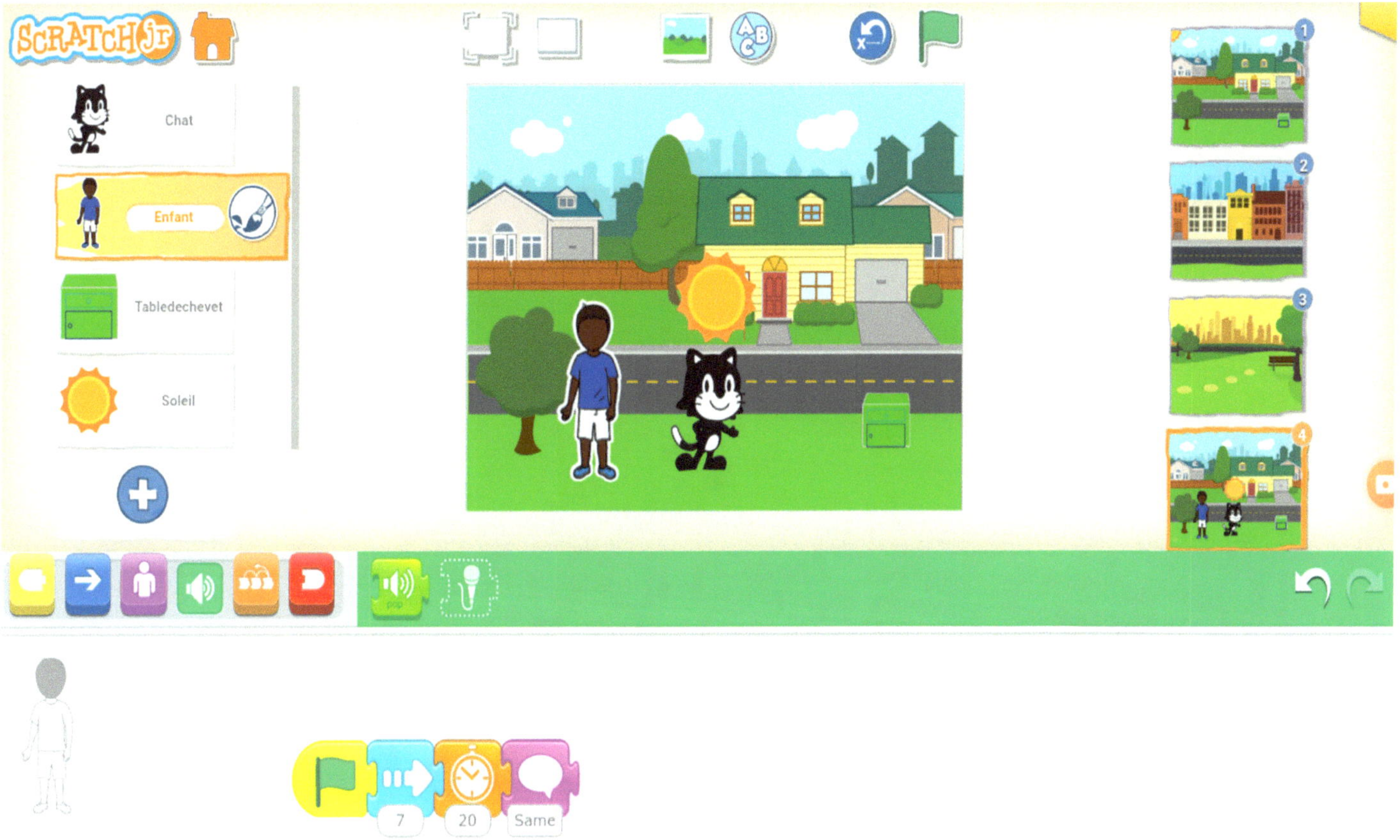

7
20
Same

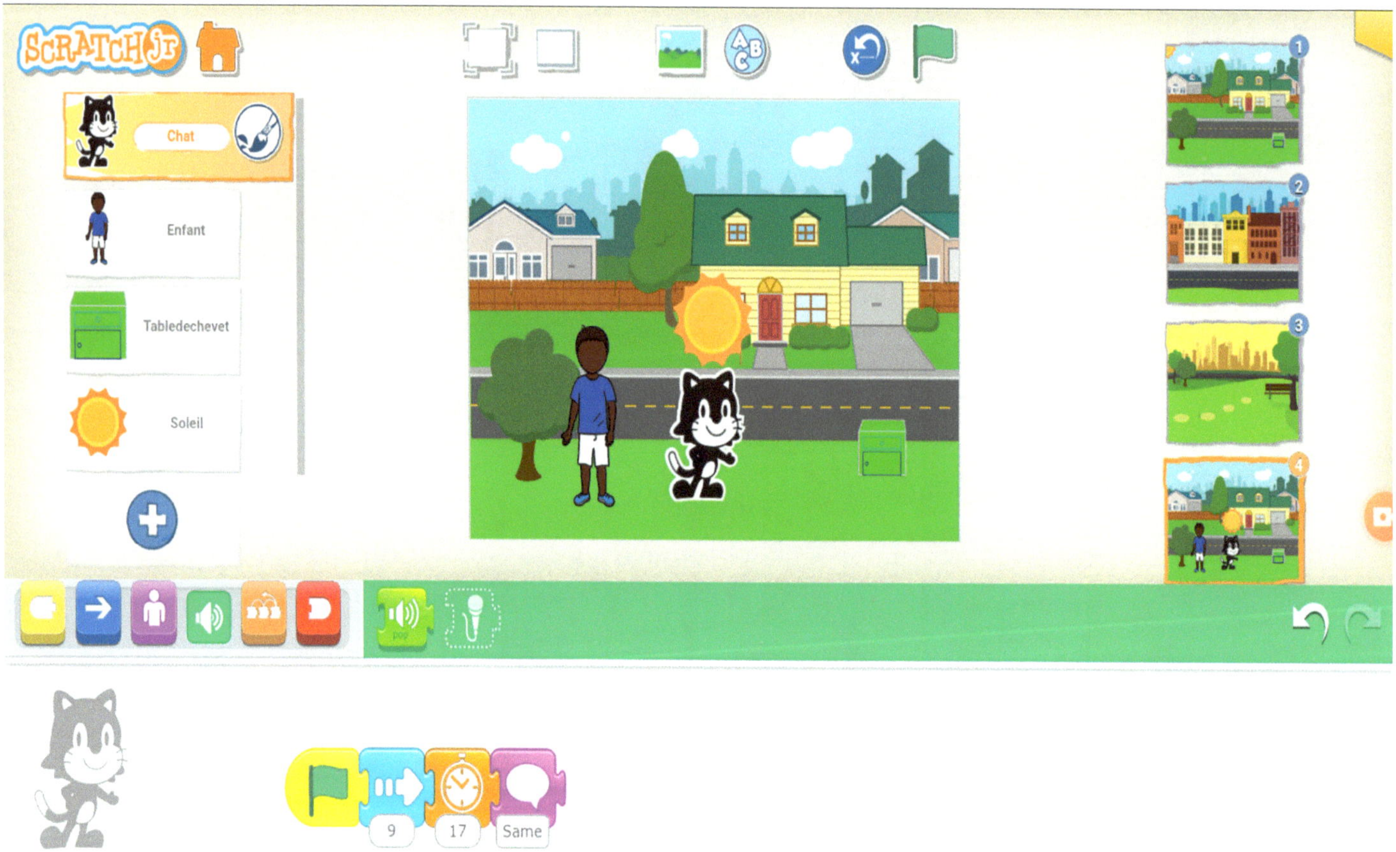

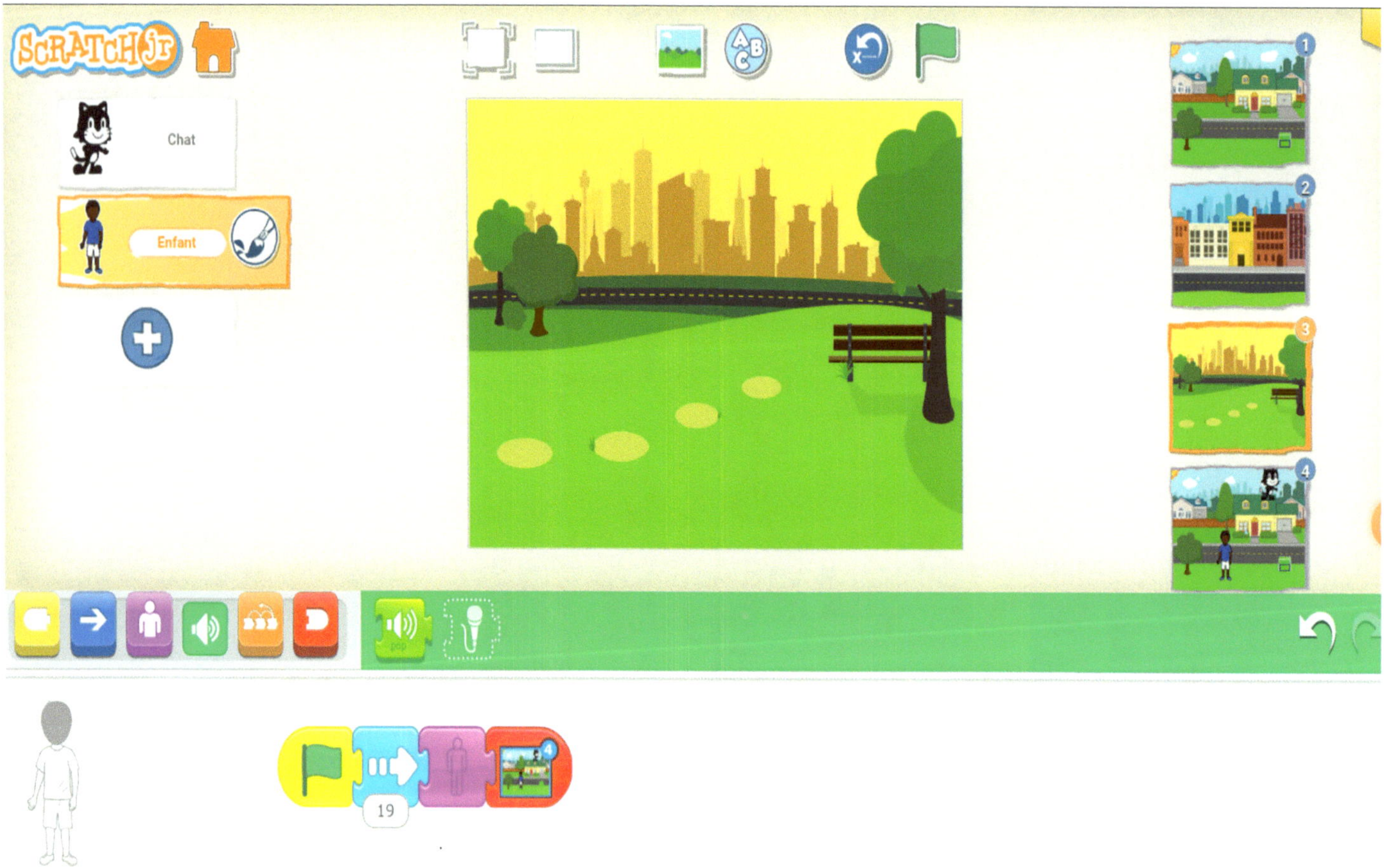

19

SCRATCH Jr
Chat
Enfant
pop
19

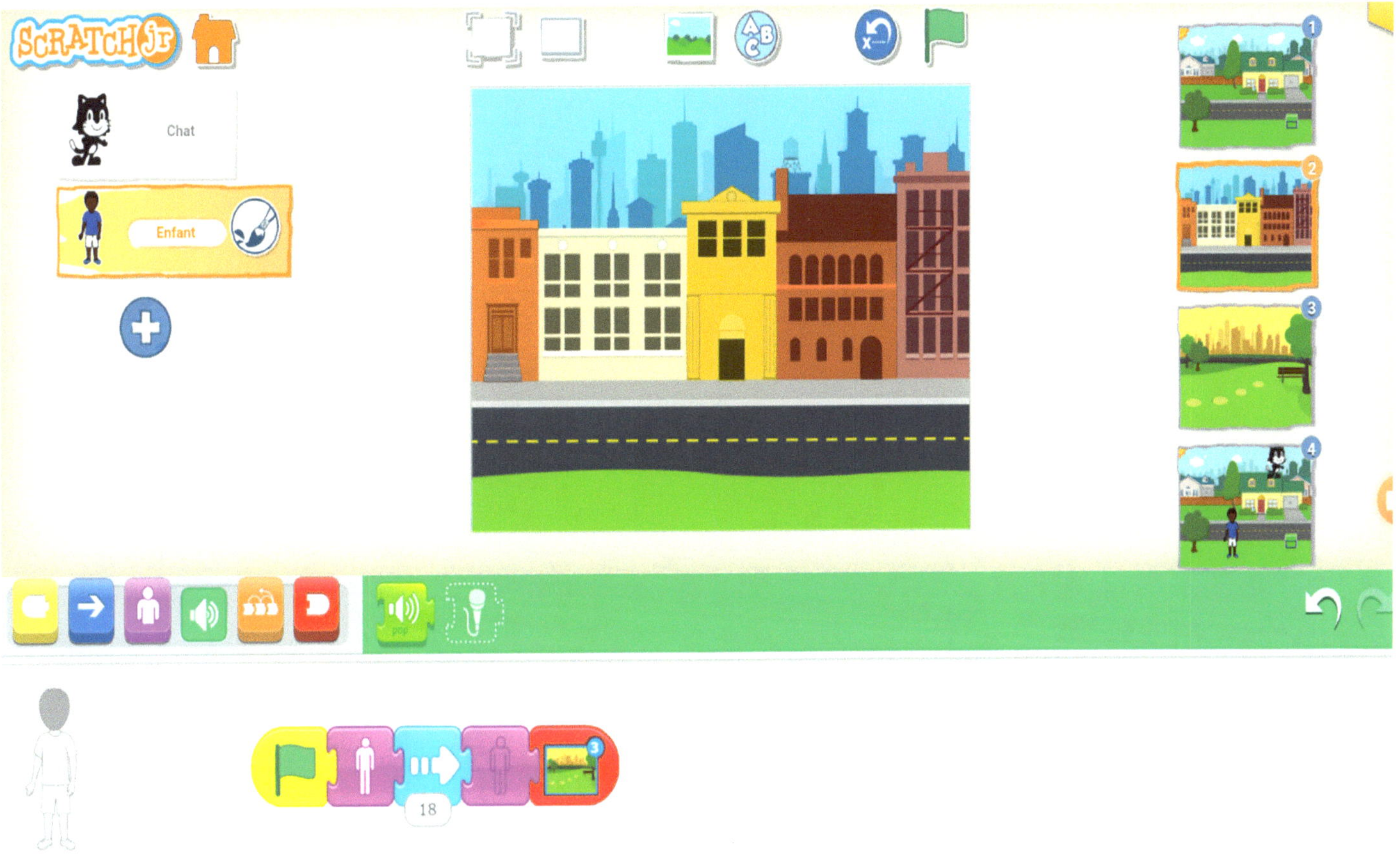

18

24

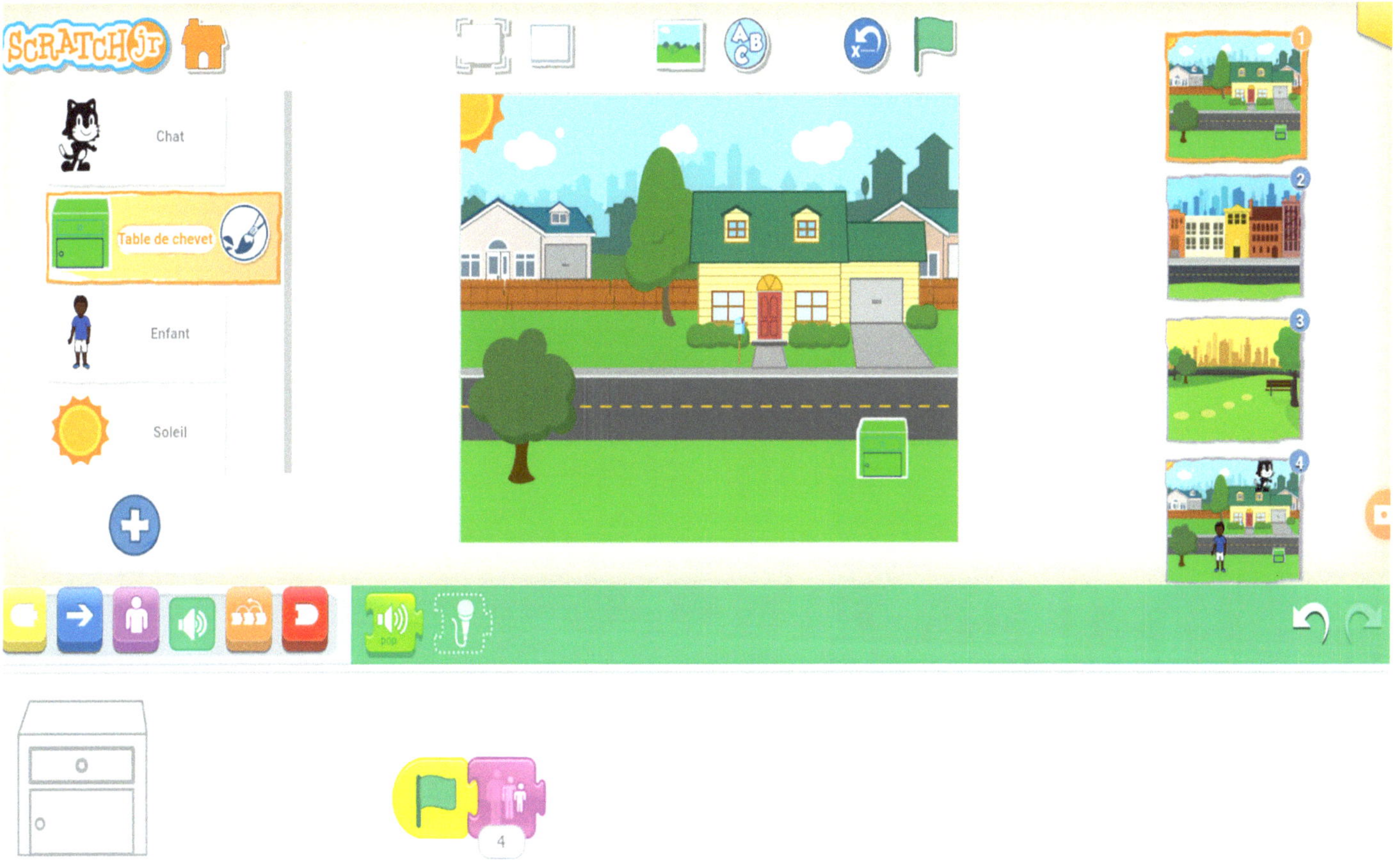

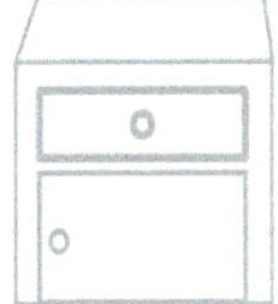

Chat

Table de chevet

Enfant

Soleil

SCRATCH Jr
Chat
Table de chevet
Enfant
Soleil
34
1
5
7
2
1
20
Excuse
5
And
20
8
2
I do
Tell me
And
20
18
Ok
9

26